50 Brilliant PE Challenges

Using Just a

Tennis Ball

Will Hussey

We hope you and your pupils enjoy using the ideas in this book. Listed below are a few of our other books which might be of interest to you. Information on these and all our other books can be found on our website: www.brilliantpublications.co.uk.

Other books in the series
50 Brilliant PE Challenges Using Just a Beanbag
50 Brilliant PE Challenges Using Just a Hoop

Other PE books
100+ Fun Ideas for Teaching PE Games
43 Team-building Activities for KS1
43 Team-building Activities for KS2
100+ Fun Ideas for Playground Games

Other books written by Will Hussey
Where Can an Elephant Hide?
Where Can an Elephant Roost?
Brilliant Activities to Stimulate Creative Thinking

Published by Brilliant Publications
Unit 10
Sparrow Hall Farm
Edlesborough
Dunstable
Bedfordshire
LU6 2ES, UK

www.brilliantpublications.co.uk

The name Brilliant Publications and the logo are registered trademarks.

Written by Will Hussey
Illustrations and cover illustration by Steph Dix

© Text Will Hussey 2015
© Design Brilliant Publications 2015
ISBN printed book: 978-1-78317-139-2
ISBN e-pdf: 978-1-78317-143-9
First printed and published in the UK in 2015

The right of Will Hussey to be identified as the author of this work has been asserted by himself in accordance with the Copyright, Designs and Patents Act 1988.

No part of this book may be reproduced in any other form or for any other purpose without the prior permission of the publisher.

Contents

Introduction 4

Individual challenges
1. Throw up 5
2. Circus school 6
3. Mirror, mirror......................7
4. Low down..........................8
5. Elbow grease 9
6. Back-hander 10
7. Long John Silver 11
8. Chicken roll......................12
9. Double up........................13
10. Triple up 14
11. Kick up 15

Group/paired challenges
12. Throw go........................16
13. Square ball 17
14. Marbles..........................18
15. French cricket 19
16. Golf................................20
17. Earthworks 21
18. Fireworks 22
19. Loaded 23
20. Wimbledon....................24
21. Three little pigs...............25
22. Rebound........................26
23. Knife edge 27
24. Catching fire 28
25. Sweet pea 29

26. Back-handed..................30
27. Push ha'penny 31
28. Kick start........................32
29. Pendulum 33
30. Bread crumbs.................34
31. Duel...............................35
32. Quarterback 36
33. Backfire 37

Class challenges
34. Potato pass 38
35. Knuckle down 39
36. Bowled over 40
37. Hopping mad.................41
38. Pecking order.................42
39. Picking order 43
40. Game of throws.............44
41. Jump start......................45
42. Ace shuttle 46
43. Eliminator 47
44. Chain gang 48
45. Outer space 49
46. Pass out........................50
47. Ring of steel..................51
48. Pin ball..........................52
49. Beacon 53
50. Snake 54

Index (by level of difficulty)...55

50 Brilliant PE Challenges Using Just a Tennis Ball

Introduction

50 Brilliant PE Challenges Using Just a Tennis Ball does exactly what it says on the tin.

This handy teacher resource will provide a wealth of active and enjoyable activities, inspiring outstanding learning with minimal preparation.

A mixture of differentiated individual, group and whole class activities, with suggestions for further challenge and extension, ensures the busy teacher can create bespoke lessons.

The **50 Brilliant PE Challenges** series of books believes less is more: inclusive competition and engagement facilitated by minimal preparation and resources regardless of subject expertise. Brilliant challenges create brilliant PE lessons!

Key

👤	Individual challenge
👥👥👥	Group/paired challenge
👥👥👥👥👥	Whole class challenge
☆	Moderate difficulty
☆☆	Intermediate
☆☆☆	Advanced

1. Throw up

Challenge

Children should see how high they can throw a ball and catch it, whilst both feet remain planted in the same position throughout.

Tip
Begin with a relatively modest throw and gradually increase the height after every successful catch.

Development
Progress from catching with two hands to catching with one hand – and then the other hand.

2. Circus school

Challenge

Children should throw and catch the ball between the palms of their hands, crossing over their forearms to create a 'pincer' movement.

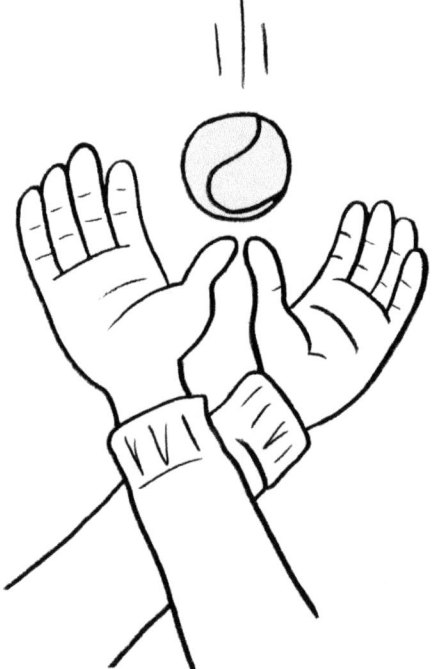

Tip
Keeping the arms extended in front helps to facilitate the required catching action.

Development
Throw and catch the ball with or without a bounce, ask a friend to throw the ball, or try catching the ball after it rebounds off a wall.

3. Mirror, mirror

> **Challenge**
> Children should prepare themselves to throw the ball above their head, before rotating their bodies 180° to catch the ball in a mirror-image of their starting position.

Tip
Movement of the legs and body should take place after the initial throw and prior to the ball being caught.

Development
Encourage the children to rotate a full 360° if deemed appropriate, or use a line to transcend; increasing the distance between throwing and catching positions.

4. Low down

> **Challenge**
> Try to pat the tennis ball continuously as though it is a basketball, bouncing the ball closer and closer to the ground whilst maintaining control.

Tip
This activity typically goes awry when the tennis ball bounces lowest to the ground; try to increase the amount of force applied and return to the starting position.

Development
Suggest that participants must first sit and then lie on the ground whilst maintaining control of the bouncing, before returning to a standing position.

5. Elbow grease

Challenge

Hold the ball in one hand in front, as if about to take a bite from an apple. Let go of the ball and extend the arm simultaneously, hitting the ball with the upside of the elbow before catching with the same arm.

Tip
Simply release the tennis ball, rather than trying to throw it in any particular direction. The success of this task relies on it being executed in one quick action.

Development
Catch with the opposite hand to which the ball is released, or catch low in 'back-hander' fashion (see Challenge no. 6).

6. Back-hander

> **Challenge**
> Children endeavour to catch the ball one-handed, with their arm extended vertically by their side and palm facing upwards.

Tip
Careful footwork is required to ensure that the whole of the body is correctly positioned; do not allow the arm to 'detach' from the side.

Development:
The tennis ball can be bounced prior to catching, or alternatively a friend can throw the ball to be caught.

7. Long John Silver ☆☆☆

Challenge
Encourage the children to throw the ball so it bounces vertically, and position themselves to try to catch the descending ball behind them in the crook of a bent knee.

Tip
It is easier to position the body in preparation for the 'catch' if the ball descends vertically, rather than at a slight angle.

Development
Try catching the ball without a prior bounce, or try to use the other 'weaker' leg to catch with.

---

50 Brilliant PE Challenges Using Just a Tennis Ball

8. Chicken roll

> **Challenge**
> The children should try to throw the ball a little way above their head, before watching the ball descend carefully and endeavouring to cushion it between the back of the neck and the shoulder blades.

Tip
Watching the ball drop until the last possible moment helps position the body effectively.

Development
The higher the ball is thrown the more challenging this activity is to complete. The ball can also be kicked into the air prior to catching to create additional difficulty.

9. Double up

Challenge

Place one arm behind the back, and use the other hand to try to juggle two tennis balls.

Tip
One tennis ball should be thrown in the same action as catching the next.

Development
Attempt to throw the tennis balls higher and lower whilst continuing the juggling action.

10. Triple up

Challenge

Try to juggle three balls at once, making sure there is never more than one ball in a hand at any time (apart from when initiating the activity.)

Tip
Start with two tennis balls in one hand, throwing one just above head height. Catch this ball with the opposite hand, having released the other tennis ball in the process. Continue this dual action of throwing and catching to juggle three balls at a time.

Development
Once mastered the same activity can be undertaken rebounding the tennis balls off a wall.

11. Kick up

Challenge

One player attempts to kick the ball vertically in to the air, allowing it to drop and bounce before repeating the action, thus initiating a rally. How many kicks can the player manage in succession?

Tip
Try to eliminate some of the bounces in between kick-ups, so the ball has minimal contact with the ground.

Development
Both players endeavour to continue the rally by kicking the ball to each other, allowing one bounce each pass.

50 Brilliant PE Challenges Using Just a Tennis Ball   15

12. Throw go

Challenge

Working in pairs, pupils should try to make the maximum number of passes possible within a given time limit. They are not allowed to place the ball in their opponent's hand.

Tip
Sometimes standing too close to a partner can inhibit the passing action; positioning a pace apart can be beneficial for some.

Development
Stipulate the distance apart that certain pairs have to stand, or suggest an action that must be undertaken after every throw (such as touching the floor).

13. Square ball

> **Challenge**
>
> This is an activity for two teams each of four children. One team stands in a square formation and tries to pass the ball around as many sides as possible. Meanwhile the other team runs relay fashion around the square. When the 'runners' have each completed a lap of the square the passing must stop. The teams swap over; the winner being the team with the most passes.

Tip
The team running around the square should carry a tennis ball, which they then relay instead of a baton.

Development
Increase the size of the square or suggest an additional action after each pass has been completed (such as turning 360°.)

14. Marbles

> **Challenge**
> Two children begin the game by standing side by side. One child rolls their ball some distance away. The other decides to either attempt to hit their opponent's ball, or alternatively play 'safe,' by rolling away. Players take turns; the winner being the first to hit the other's tennis ball.

Tip
Rolling the tennis ball seems generally more accurate than throwing it.

Development
Playing in groups of three or four adds further challenge.

15. French cricket

Challenge

A child uses his hand as a bat, trying to defend the area below his knees – the wicket. The rest of the players attempt to catch the batsman out or alternatively bowl the 'wicket' area. Should the batsman move their feet at any time they are also judged to be out. Fielders bowl the ball from where it rests or they manage to stop it.

Tip
Fielders can throw the ball to someone better placed to bowl if they so choose.

Development
The batsman can score 'runs' by completing star jumps every time he has the opportunity after hitting the ball. He must, however, have regained the 'wicket' position prior to the next bowl or he is 'out' by default.

16. Golf

Challenge

Roll out a tennis ball into a large space to indicate the 'hole'. Children take it in turns to try to find the hole by throwing or rolling their tennis ball towards it. The winner is the player who takes the least number of shots to locate it. Take it in turns to position the next 'hole'.

Tip
This game is most effective when played over a distance requiring a minimum of four or five shots.

Development
Encourage the children to record the number of shots taken, providing a winner at the end of the round. Players enjoy considering a 'par' for the course.

50 Brilliant PE Challenges Using Just a Tennis Ball

17. Earthworks

Challenge

A pair of children take turns to throw the ball, attempting to be the first team to cover an agreed distance. The ball must have stopped rolling before the other partner can retrieve it and throw again from a sitting position.

Tip
Suggest both children must be seated before the ball can be thrown.

Development
Stipulate that additional exercises should be carried out after the ball has stopped rolling and prior to it being thrown – such as hopping on the spot ten times, for instance.

18. Fireworks

> Children play in pairs, taking it in turns to hit their opponent's tennis ball before it falls to the ground.

Challenge

Tip
The player who aims to target their opponent's ball should ensure they actually release their own tennis ball, throwing to create a mid-air 'collision'.

Development
The second player should face the opposite direction to the person launching their tennis ball, giving a verbal instruction indicating when the ball has been thrown.

19. Loaded

Challenge

Working in groups of four/five children, they should try to facilitate one member of their team in covering a short distance whilst carrying as many tennis balls as possible. If any tennis balls drop to the ground, the attempt is invalidated.

Tip
Suggest that a different team member takes their turn after each attempt.

Development
Pairs of children could try the same activity, balancing the tennis balls collaboratively.

20. Wimbledon

Challenge
Children endeavour to continue a rally by 'hitting,' the tennis ball back and forth with the palm of their hand.

Tip
Remind the children that they can use either hand. Keep the fingers closed with a degree of tension to avoid 'catching' the ball.

Development
Stipulate that the ball is not allowed above shoulder height, requiring greater control and accuracy.

21. Three little pigs

Challenge

Each child takes a turn at being the 'piggy,' in the middle whilst the others endeavour to keep the tennis ball away from them. Should the piggy touch the ball or one of the players whilst in possession of the ball, then roles are swapped.

Tip
Suggest the children play within designated parameters and are not allowed to 'travel' in possession of the tennis ball.

Development
Throw and catch the ball with one hand only, or perhaps 'bounce pass' to each other.

22. Rebound

Challenge
Pairs of children each throw a tennis ball in the direction of their partner, attempting to make the balls collide and rebound before catching them again. The winning pair achieves the most catches in the time available.

Tip
Throwing the ball underarm in unison helps to achieve a measured rebound.

Development
Introduce a third player, thus trying to rebound and catch three tennis balls simultaneously.

23. Knife edge

Challenge

Select two children to roll their tennis balls in approximately the same direction. Ask the rest of the group to imagine there was a straight line drawn between these two balls. They should attempt to roll their tennis balls as close as possible to the imaginary line. The two attempts deemed closest begin the next game.

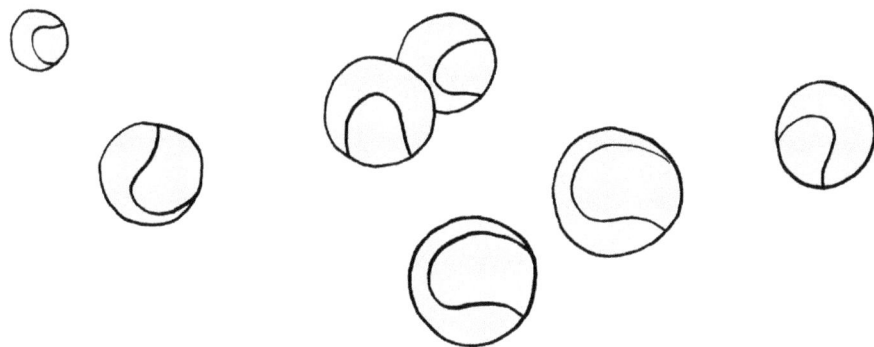

Tip
Rolling the tennis balls is generally less erratic than throwing them.

Development
Stipulate that tennis balls are not allowed to make contact; this results in a player automatically being disqualified from that particular game.

24. Catching fire

> **Challenge**
> Five children organise themselves in a semi-circle with a sixth child positioned in the middle. The central child sends the ball to any of the other children who must field and return the ball as quickly and accurately as possible.

Tip
Children need to be spaced so that the ball is unlikely to breach the fielders.

Development
The central child stipulates an action to be completed each time the ball is fielded.

25. Sweet pea

Challenge

Pairs of children sit back to back with a tennis ball suspended between them. They must endeavour to stand without the ball dropping to the floor.

Tip
Participants should start with their legs outstretched in front of them. Hands are not permitted to touch the floor.

Development
If successful, children can try to sit down again and repeat the challenge without repositioning the tennis ball.

50 Brilliant PE Challenges Using Just a Tennis Ball

26. Back-handed

> **Challenge**
> Playing in pairs, they begin by facing each other holding the tennis ball in their left hand. They attempt to throw their tennis balls toward their partner and simultaneously catch their partner's. Try continuing the passing in this way without dropping a ball.

Tip
Children should try to direct their tennis ball to the appropriate side of their partner, making it easier for both parties to catch.

Development
Extend the distance over which the tennis balls are being thrown, or introduce a time limit for completing the most number of passes.

27. Push ha'penny

Challenge
Players from two opposing teams take it in turns to try to 'push' a centrally positioned ball in the direction of the opposition, throwing tennis balls to cannon the target ball. The winning team succeeds in moving the game ball over an agreed point.

Tip
Ensure only one player aims a ball at a time, alternating between each team.

Development
Stipulate that players should throw either under or over arm. Increase the distance the target ball is required to be 'pushed' or suggest 'weaker' hands should be used.

28. Kick start

Challenge

One player bounces the tennis ball to their partner, who attempts to return the ball by kicking with the instep of the foot. Players swap roles after completing ten passes.

Tip
Delivery of the ball must be carefully weighted, ensuring it does not bounce too high or too quickly.

Development
Continue the action to form a rally, with both players returning the ball by kicking it.

29. Pendulum

Challenge

Work with a partner to continually pass a single tennis ball without dropping it. Begin by one player throwing with their left hand to their friend's left hand, who in turn returns to their partner's right. How many passes can be sent and received by alternating the hand every time?

Tip
Try to establish a steady rhythm, without throwing the ball too high or far.

Development
Try bouncing the tennis balls to each other, or alternating a direct throw with a bounce.

30. Bread crumbs

Challenge

The group works together to perpetuate a circular trail, where the person at the back of the line runs to the front and puts down their tennis ball. The person now at the back must pick up the next ball they come across, before running to the front of the line and the process continues.

Tip
The members of the line should allow sufficient space between them and pace themselves carefully.

Development
Suggest the children try to form a figure-of-eight trail, or reverse direction midway.

31. Duel

Challenge
A pair of competing children start back-to-back, with a tennis ball placed by their feet. They both walk ten paces away, counting aloud as they do so. After the tenth pace has been completed, both children turn and endeavour to hit the stationary ball with their own tennis ball. They can continue to throw their ball from where it comes to rest, until the target is successfully hit.

Tip
Accuracy is more important than speed; take time in aiming and try not to overthrow the ball.

Development
Ask a third party to place the target ball in an alternative position as both players walk in the opposite direction.

32. Quarterback

> **Challenge**
> This is a collaborative challenge for two players. Both participants begin by standing side by side. One player runs away, and the other attempts to throw the ball over his partner's shoulder, for his partner to catch mid-stride.

Tip
Players should agree upon a signal for indicating when the tennis ball is thrown.

Development
Increase the distance the ball is required to be thrown before catching.

33. Backfire

Challenge
Standing back to back with a partner, players attempt to throw the ball over head for their partner to catch.

Tip
Agree upon a verbal signal for indicating when the ball is thrown.

Development
Suggest that participants introduce a gap between them; increasing the size of the gap will further add to the level of difficulty.

34. Potato pass

Teams compete against each other to transfer the ball over a set distance, taking it in turns to receive the ball. Players must remain stationary when in possession of the ball and only move forward when not in possession. The whole team must return to the beginning if the ball is dropped.

Challenge

Tip
Try to throw accurately rather than over long distances; team mates should be in position ready to field the ball as soon as the previous team member has received it.

Development
Insist children use just one hand to catch with – and then the other hand!

35. Knuckle down

Challenge

Teams of two children race to transport a tennis ball over a predetermined distance, with the ball sandwiched between a clenched fist from each partner. Players must return to the start if they drop the ball.

Tip
Run alongside next to your partner rather than in front or behind.

Development
Attempt this challenge using the other 'weaker' hand.

36. Bowled over

> **Challenge**
> Split the class into two competing teams. One half positions themselves with legs fixed shoulder width apart. The other team tries to eliminate them by rolling a tennis ball between their feet.

Tip
The bowling team should all throw from one side before swapping to bowl from the opposite direction. Compete to see which team is eliminated in the least number of 'ends'.

Development
Implement a time limit or narrow the gap between the targets' feet.

37. Hopping mad

Challenge
Relay teams compete in a hopping race, but each participant must clamp a tennis ball between their bent leg.

Tip
Position the tennis ball as close as possible to the crook of the knee.

Development
Insist team members 'swap' legs half way through.

38. Pecking order

> The class jog around in a large rectangle, picking up a tennis ball or alternatively putting one down when the teacher blows a whistle.

Challenge

Tip
Participants should try to remain evenly spaced and proceed at a pace accessible to all.

Development
On the teacher's instruction children should change direction.

39. Picking order

Challenge

Relay teams compete to gather the most tennis balls, participants taking it in turns to retrieve one at a time.

Tip
Ensure the tennis balls are well spread out, minimising the likelihood of collision.

Development
Mark some of the tennis balls to differentiate them; award 'double points,' for each.

40. Game of throws

Challenge

The class attempt to avoid several participants chosen to be 'it'. These players endeavour to throw a tennis ball underarm to hit competitors below the knee – rendering them 'stuck' in a star shape. They can be released should someone run under their outstretched arm.

Tip
Suggest the ball must hit the ground before making contact with a player.

Development
Alternatively, when a player is 'stuck', they should swap roles with the person who targeted them and take their turn at being 'on'.

41. Jump start

Challenge

Teams compete to be the first to complete a relay race; jumping two-footed with a tennis ball squashed between their knees. Should the tennis ball become dislodged, participants must stop and reposition it before continuing.

Tip
A little control is required – smaller jumps are typically more effective than larger exertions.

Development
Suggest that if a player drops the ball, they must go back to the start line.

42. Ace shuttle

> Relay teams compete to either pick up or put down three tennis balls at varying intervals. The first player retrieves the first ball, returning the ball to the start before repeating for the remaining two. The next team member replaces the balls one at a time for the following participant to retrieve and so on.

Challenge

Tip
Tennis balls can be picked up or put down in any order; furthest from or nearest to the starting point according to preference.

Development
Increase the distance over which the tennis balls are spaced, either for all players or just to handicap selected teams.

43. Eliminator

Challenge

All participants must throw their tennis balls vertically in to the air when instructed, endeavouring to catch them. Anyone who drops the ball is automatically eliminated from the game, as is the player who is deemed to throw their ball lower than anyone else.

Tip
All players must throw their ball when instructed; hesitation leads to disqualification.

Development
Try the activity catching with one hand only – and then the other hand.

44. Chain gang

Challenge
Teams of children position themselves evenly spaced across a divide, with the aim of transferring a given number of tennis balls along the line in the shortest possible time. Any tennis balls that are dropped must be rolled back to the beginning of the chain. The first team to transfer all the tennis balls wins.

Tip
Ensure that players do not throw the ball until the next person in line is ready to receive it.

Development
Stipulate that players must catch with one hand (and then the other). Alternatively increase the distance over which the tennis balls must be transferred, with the person at the back of the link able to run around to the front.

50 Brilliant PE Challenges Using Just a Tennis Ball

45. Outer space

Challenge

Fifteen tennis balls are clustered together in the middle of a large circle formed by class members. The children try to displace the positioned tennis balls by throwing or rolling additional balls from the edge of the circle... the aim is to displace the tennis balls in the shortest possible time.

Tip
Limit the number of tennis balls to be thrown to approximately half of the number of people throwing them.

Development
Make the circle larger, making it more difficult to field the thrown tennis balls and target those positioned in the middle.

46. Pass out

> **Challenge**
> Participants form a circle. On the teacher's command they try to pass their tennis ball to the person on their left whilst catching the incoming tennis ball from their right. Children who fail to catch the ball are eliminated from the circle.

Tip
Emphasise that players must 'deliver' their pass with a reasonable degree of control and accuracy.

Development
Stipulate that players may only use one hand to throw and catch – and then their least preferred hand.

47. Ring of steel

Challenge
Two chosen members of the class stand inside a circle of thirty tennis balls, approximately five metres in diameter. They endeavour to clear the circle of tennis balls faster than the rest of the class can return them.

Tip
The pair 'clearing' the circle can only throw the tennis balls underarm, and children returning the tennis balls must place them (rather than throw them).

Development
Differentiate the size of the circle to be cleared, the number of tennis balls used or the amount of people 'clearing' or retrieving the tennis balls.

48. Pin ball

Challenge
Two thirds of the class position themselves stationary ready to receive the ball. Five children must try and throw the ball to (and receive a return pass from) as many of these 'pins' as possible so as to eliminate them from the playing area before the remainder of the children manage to intercept the pass by catching or touching the ball (causing the 'pin ball' player to exit the game.)

Tip
Ensure the class swap and rotate the roles.

Development
Increasing or decreasing the amount of pins, or pursuers, changes the dynamic of the game.

49. Beacon

Challenge

The class work collaboratively to position themselves as wide apart as possible, whilst able to throw the ball along the line without it being dropped. Every player must be included: how far can the ball be transported in this manner?

Tip
Classes that become proficient at this may effectively 'lap' the playground or field.

Development
How far can the line stretch if players are only allowed to catch with one hand? How fast can the ball be transported along the line?

50. Snake

Challenge

Children attempt to travel in the longest possible chain, holding a ball in each hand and suspending an additional one between themselves and the next person. Adjacent players are therefore connected by transporting three tennis balls.

Tip
This activity is sometimes best introduced by asking children to move in a line holding a tennis ball in each hand, ensuring contact is maintained between adjacent participants.

Development
Introduce obstacles to be overcome or derive a challenging route to be navigated in a limited amount of time.

Index (by level of difficulty)

Page

Moderate difficulty
12. Throw go 16
13. Square ball 17
14. Marbles 18
15. French cricket 19
16. Golf....................................20
17. Earthworks 21
34. Potato pass 38
35. Knuckle down 39
36. Bowled over 40
37. Hopping mad...................41
38. Pecking order..................42
39. Picking order 43
40. Game of throws...............44
41. Jump start.......................45
42. Ace shuttle 46
43. Eliminator 47

Intermediate
1. Throw up 5
2. Circus school 6
3. Mirror, mirror......................7
4. Low down 8
5. Elbow grease 9
18. Fireworks 22
19. Loaded 23
20. Wimbledon.......................24

21. Three little pigs.................25
22. Rebound 26
23. Knife edge 27
24. Catching fire 28
25. Sweet pea 29
26. Back-handed 30
27. Push ha'penny 31
28. Kick start..........................32
44. Chain gang 48
45. Outer space 49
46. Pass out..........................50
47. Ring of steel....................51
48. Pin ball............................52

Advanced
6. Back-hander 10
7. Long John Silver 11
8. Chicken roll......................12
9. Double up........................13
10. Triple up 14
11. Kick up 15
29. Pendulum 33
30. Bread crumbs.................34
31. Duel 35
32. Quarterback 36
33. Backfire 37
49. Beacon 53
50. Snake 54

50 Brilliant PE Challenges Using Just a Tennis Ball

Milton Keynes UK
Ingram Content Group UK Ltd.
UKHW020201110424
440921UK00010B/236